Training Pablo

written by Wendy Graham

illustrated by Peggy Mozley

Engage Literacy is published in 2013 by Raintree.
Raintree is an imprint of Capstone Global Library Limited, a company incorporated in Engand and Wales having its registered office at 7 Pilgrim Street, London, EC4V 6LB – Registered company number: 6695582
www.raintreepublishers.co.uk

Originally published in Australia by Hinkler Education, a division of Hinkler Books Pty Ltd.
Text copyright © Wendy Graham 2012
Illustration copyright © Hinkler Books Pty Ltd 2012

Written by Wendy Graham
Lead authors Jay Dale and Anne Giulieri
Cover illustration and illustrations by Peggy Mozley
Edited by Gwenda Smyth
UK edition edited by Dan Nunn, Catherine Veitch and Sian Smith
Designed by Susannah Low, Butterflyrocket Design

All rights reserved. No part of this publication may be reproduced, stored in a retrieval system, or transmitted in any way or by any means, electronic, mechanical, photocopying, recording or otherwise, without the prior written permission of Capstone Global Library Limited.

Training Pablo
ISBN: 978 1 406 26540 8
10 9 8 7 6 5 4 3 2 1

Printed and bound in China by Leo Paper Products Ltd

Contents

Chapter 1	Happy Birthday	4
Chapter 2	Lessons for Pablo	8
Chapter 3	Pablo Gets Out!	14
Chapter 4	Colin Has an Idea	18

Chapter 1
Happy Birthday

"Happy Birthday, Colin!"
Mum smiled as she placed
a bright red birdcage on the table.

Colin couldn't believe his eyes.
Inside the birdcage was a beautiful green
and yellow parakeet.

"He's only ten weeks old," said Mum.
"You'll be able to teach him to talk."

"Thank you, Mum," said Colin, happily. Then he carefully put his finger into the cage. The parakeet flapped his wings in fright.

"Come on, little bird," said Colin, gently.
"You don't need to be frightened of me."
Then Colin moved a little bit closer
and whistled a tune.
The parakeet moved his head to listen.
"I'm going to call you Pablo," smiled Colin.
"Pablo the parakeet!"

Chapter 2
Lessons for Pablo

The next day, Colin read about training pet parakeets.
He read everything he could
and began Pablo's training straight away.

In one week, Pablo had learned to step
onto Colin's finger and to eat from his hand.
The following week, he had learned
to perch on his shoulder.
Pablo loved to hear Colin whistle.
Whenever he heard the little tune,
he would fly over and perch
on Colin's shoulder.
Then he would sit very still and listen.

Sometimes Pablo perched on Colin's shoulder when he ate his dinner.
One evening, Pablo fluttered down to Colin's plate and took a little bite of his carrot.
Mum wasn't happy at all!
"Put that bird back in his cage," she said to Colin.
"He nearly landed in your glass of milk!"

Colin also began to teach Pablo to talk.
While Pablo was perched on his shoulder,
Colin said a few words over and over.
"Cheeky boy, Pablo.
Cheeky boy, Pablo."
He hoped that one day
Pablo would talk back!

Pablo quickly became part of the family.
Colin and Mum allowed him to fly
all around the house,
but only when the doors
and windows were shut!

The little parakeet loved to play games, too.
He quickly learned how to play
with a bead counter.
He learned how to push the beads along,
one by one, with his beak.

Pablo also learned to pick up coins
from the table, and carry them to the side.
Then he would toss them over, looking down
to see where they had landed.

Colin noticed that Pablo had been making some funny squeaking noises.

This meant that Pablo was getting ready to talk.

So Colin kept saying, "Cheeky boy, Pablo. Cheeky boy, Pablo" over and over.

He hoped that Pablo would talk very soon.

Pablo was the perfect pet parakeet!

Chapter 3
Pablo Gets Out!

Then a terrible thing happened.
One day, after school, Colin opened the back door to come inside.
Pablo was waiting for him.
He flew down towards Colin's shoulder, but then he flew straight out the door!
He landed on the branch of a tree.

"Oh, no!" cried Colin, his heart racing. "Pablo! Pablo! Please come down."
Pablo peered down but he didn't move from the branch.

Colin didn't know what to do.
What if Pablo flew away
and never came back?
What if he was lost forever?
Colin had to think.
He couldn't climb the tree
because it was too dangerous.
And he couldn't use a ladder
because they didn't have one.

"I could stand on a chair," said Mum,
"and try to reach Pablo."

So Colin got a chair from the kitchen
and placed it beneath the tree.
Mum stood on the chair,
holding the tree trunk with one arm.
Then she reached up with her other arm
to try to get Pablo.

Mum was just about to grab Pablo when he flapped his wings and flew to another branch.
"Oh, no!" said Colin.
"Pablo thinks this is a game."

Chapter 4
Colin Has an Idea

Then Colin had an idea.
"Maybe Pablo will come down if we get some of his favourite food," he said.

"He might," agreed Mum.
"You stay here and keep an eye on him while I get some seed."
Mum raced inside and put some seed into a bowl.

When she returned, Colin held up the bowl and called, "Look, Pablo!
I've got some yummy seed for you.
Please come down, Pablo. **Please!**"
But Pablo didn't come down.
He just moved his head to the side.

Colin and Mum had to think again.

"What else might bring Pablo down?" asked Mum.

"Maybe some apple," replied Colin. "Pablo loves apple."

So this time, Mum cut up some apple and put it into the bowl as well.

"Come down, Pablo," called Colin. "Please come down."
Pablo peered down at the bowl, but he didn't move from the branch. He just sat there, looking quite happy and chirping loudly.

Colin was really worried now.
What if he never got Pablo back?
What if Pablo flew away?
"There must be something else we could try,"
said Colin, sadly.

Then he had another idea!
Why hadn't he thought of it before?
"If I whistle to Pablo," said Colin,
"he might fly down and perch
on my shoulder."

Colin began whistling.
He whistled Pablo's favourite tune.
Pablo moved his head.
He peered down at Colin.
Then all of a sudden, he flapped his wings
and flew out of the tree...

…and onto Colin's shoulder.
Colin's idea had worked!
"You gave me the biggest fright ever," said Colin, smiling at Pablo as they all quickly went inside.

"Cheeky boy, Pablo.
Cheeky boy, Pablo," replied the parakeet.